Christ for Post-Christians

Christ for Post-Christians

A Radical Shift for the Small Group Bible Study

Fred McRae

Foreword by Gundolf Lange

WIPF & STOCK · Eugene, Oregon

CHRIST FOR POST-CHRISTIANS
A Radical Shift for the Small Group Bible Study

Copyright © 2015 Fred McRae. All rights reserved. Except for brief quotations in critical publications or reviews, no part of this book may be reproduced in any manner without prior written permission from the publisher. Write: Permissions, Wipf and Stock Publishers, 199 W. 8th Ave., Suite 3, Eugene, OR 97401.

Wipf & Stock
An Imprint of Wipf and Stock Publishers
199 W. 8th Ave., Suite 3
Eugene, OR 97401

www.wipfandstock.com

ISBN 13: 978-1-4982-2372-0

Manufactured in the U.S.A.   10/12/2015

Contents

Foreword by Gundolf Lange • vii
Introduction: Why Another Book on Leading Small Groups? • ix

1. The Importance of Small Groups • 1
2. Bible Study for the Post-Christian • 8
3. Inviting Participants • 18
4. The Role of the Discussion Group Leader • 26
5. Developing Good Questions • 33
6. Explaining Evangelism • 45
7. Launching a Discussion Group—an Action Plan • 52
8. The Church and Post-Christians • 55

Foreword

Small groups (*Hausbibelkreise*) became popular in Germany in the 1980s. Besides Bible studies in a large group with a Bible teacher, the desire for small, intimate, and personal groups also increased within the churches. Sharing of and praying for individual needs, discussing biblical and personal topics, mutual support and encouragement in private homes often started with a common meal. These groups helped Christians to grow towards a more mature faith.

In the 1990s, the small group concept was adapted for people who were not yet Christians, but who were interested in the Christian faith. For them, traditional evangelism methods and church services were strange and incomprehensible. By starting post-Christian Bible discussion groups, non-Christian friends could address their questions in an intimate atmosphere. The focus in these groups was not to give a lecture on Christian topics, but to start a conversation with one another. A few Christians among the non-Christian participants could tell how their faith in Jesus affects their lives. Although designed for several weeks, sometimes the group stayed together for a much longer time. In addition, non-Christian friends attended the church service and, finally, some of them became strong Christian disciples.

Within the past several years, such post-Christian Bible discussion groups have become more important as many refugees from crisis regions such as Afghanistan, Iran, and Syria

Foreword

seek asylum in Germany. Many of them escape from their home country because the suppression through fanatic Islamic groups, like the Taliban, becomes unbearable. If they get in contact with Christians in the host country, they experience the liberating force of the gospel. But they usually know very little about the content of the Christian faith and its basic context. For those people coming from a different cultural background, post-Christian Bible discussion groups offer an excellent opportunity to lay the foundations for the Christian faith.

Due to their hospitality, the Middle Eastern people love to host a group in their home. For the "leader" of the group, there is not much preparation to do: identify relevant topics, compile respective biblical passages, und develop five to six open questions that lead to a personal discussion. Nevertheless, it is a huge challenge to cope with a different language and culture, as well as the Islamic background. The leader of the group is a facilitator, a teacher, and a personal witness of Christian faith. He or she has to leave his or her comfort zone in order to help others discover how to live out a personal relationship with Jesus. As a consequence, these people grow in faith and attract other people from their culture to the gospel. In fact, there is almost a revival movement among the refugees from Iran and Afghanistan. They confess their faith in Jesus, are baptized, and become members of the church. In addition, the friendship and sharing life with other Christians is an excellent way of integration into their new culture. So, post-Christian Bible discussion groups are gaining importance for the future as cultural and religious diversity increases.

With this book, Dr. Fred McRae helps to establish and teach post-Christian Bible discussion groups in a practical way. He also offers the great opportunity to revive interest in sharing our faith with post-Christian people (Matthew 28:18–20).

Dr. Gundolf Lange
Elder of the Neuhofen Baptist Church
Neuhofen, Germany

Introduction

Why Another Book on Leading Small Groups?

Germany is a prime example of a post-Christian country. The situation is so bad that some are wondering if Germany was ever a Christian nation at all. One example showing how Germany stands out so well as post-Christian is found in the numbers. It can be seen in the church tax that German Catholics and Lutherans are required to pay. Yes—in order to be a member of the church you have to pay the government a church income tax. It is very easy to determine the church's influence based on the number of people paying this tax. The rolls indicate that Germans are leaving the church by the thousands.

Today German Christianity is a hollow hull of what Martin Luther envisioned. It is a stark reminder of what happens to the church when it denies the authority of the Bible and turns a blind eye to cultural change. The prevailing attitude among the general culture is that it is pretentious to view one religion as better than another. Before the 1960s, most Germans felt connected in some way to the German church; it was part of being a German. This is no longer true; the cultural connection between people and church has vanished—as the thousands who leave the church each year indicates. The land of the Reformation has become the poster child for post-Christendom, and the American church now faces this same dilemma. America is entering the post-Christian cultural phase of its history, or, as some argue, is already engulfed in it. Can we learn anything from German Christians? Are there

Introduction

universal, biblical principles we can recognize and apply to gain an evangelistic advantage in our ministries? I think so.

Although the situation in Germany is desperate, there are still many signs of life as God continues to build his church. Hundreds of churches have been planted there in the past quarter century, and compared to what Germany was forty years ago, it is an evangelist's paradise. Since 1986, I have been teaching German Christians how to evangelize their relatives, friends, and coworkers. Over the years, I have learned how to share the gospel with those who have lost any connection to authentic faith. Much of what I teach comes from years of observing growing German churches, successful German evangelists, and committed church planters. These Christians have no need to read a book on post-Christianity, or to attend a seminar explaining the culture in which they live. They have learned to adapt to their environment by discovering ways to crack the code of post-Christianity and, as second nature, to contextualize the gospel.

This book is not about your normal evangelical home Bible study. This book takes you along the path to leading an evangelistic home Bible study that is quite different from one Christians normally would attend. It is dedicated to the missiological principle that we can and should learn from Christians who live in other countries facing the same cultural barriers to the gospel as we do. If we—American Christians—are not willing to humble ourselves and admit that we do not have all the answers, then we do a disservice to those without Christ.

In Germany, I see Bible-believing churches in the last stages of existence. Entire denominations are dying out because they refuse to recognize the cultural shift that has occurred. They cling to evangelistic methods of the past, which no longer resonate among those without Christ. These churches are not liberal; they are churches in which biblical authority remains paramount. This alarms me as I think about the American church. Believing the Bible is inerrant will not magically prevent a church's demise. We must also be willing to question our evangelistic methods so as to

Introduction

be confident that our message is understood and relevant to the post-Christian culture in which we find ourselves.

The purpose of this book is to encourage the formation and growth of evangelistic Bible studies that meet the needs of post-Christians. It is my hope that those without Christ will hear and understand the gospel message, come to a living faith, and follow Christ as true disciples by serving in his church.

1

The Importance of Small Groups

Small group Bible studies have been around for centuries. Martin Luther, the German pastor and theologian, intended to lead a movement to reform the Catholic Church. However, the Reformation led to an all out rebellion and protest movement that resulted in a massive split in the Catholic Church. This gave birth to Protestantism, which ushered in the use and popularity of the small group Bible study.

As the Reformation gained a foothold in European Christianity, the tendency toward dead religious orthodoxy and rote tradition also grew. This meant that as long as you intellectually believed the church particulars of Christian doctrine, your place in the church and in heaven were secure. Christian doctrine need not affect your heart. Feelings were frowned upon, and the idea of a relationship with the Lord Jesus was foreign in those days, at least in the minds of most pastors and parishioners. Some people, however, had a real problem with the lack of any feelings, emotions, or intimacy toward God, causing them finally to do something about it. In the late 1600s some Christians, called Pietists, began to meet in homes after Sunday worship for fellowship, prayer, and Bible study. Thus the Protestant home group Bible study was born.

The small group phenomenon subsequently spread throughout Europe and eventually made its way to America.

Small groups have always been popular in the United States, but they really took off in the 1960s and 1970s. Peninsula Bible Church in Palo Alto, California, and its "body life" concept impacted churches all over the world. Fellowship Bible Church in Dallas, Texas, had a similar impact with its "mini-churches," which were home-based small group Bible studies. These two churches spawned movements that changed traditional worship services in America and around the world. Hundreds of new churches in the following decades patterned their Sunday services and church life after Peninsula Bible and Fellowship Bible.

Both of these movements came along as the traditional denominations began to loose their influence on the religious life in America. As the Pietists founded small groups to meet their need for a deeper spiritual life, disgruntled Baptists, Methodists, and Presbyterians fled to non-denominational Bible churches to quench their thirst for more Bible-centered preaching. Where there was no Bible Church, one was planted. Christians, tired of hearing evangelistic or topical preaching every Sunday, wanted biblical, expository sermons. They also recognized the necessity of small groups.

One of the universal characteristics of a healthy and growing church is the emphasis on small groups. This shows the continuing need and desire of Christians to meet together outside of Sunday mornings. Most importantly, it drives home the point that Sunday services cannot meet all the needs of Christians. However, there are some local churches that do not allow small groups. This may be hard to believe, but it is true. The reason is simple: pastors want to keep a reign on church members. These autocrats think that small groups, mini-churches, community groups, or whatever they may be called are places that breed discontent, false doctrine, and independence. Lack of small group Bible studies helps the pastor exert tighter control over the congregation.

Small groups are a part of Protestant history and are here to stay. They provide what the Sunday morning service cannot:

intimacy. Masks come off, hurts are laid bare, doubts surface. God becomes real. We see his love fleshed out in the care and concern shown us from other flawed and struggling people. Spiritual growth occurs and people become true disciples of Christ. From this point on, I will refer to these types of small groups as *discipleship groups*. Discipleship groups are very similar to one another, no matter where they are located on the evangelical map, no matter which denomination.

With the above characteristics in view, it is obvious that small groups can be a great platform for evangelistic outreach. Many non-Christians would not feel comfortable in a Sunday morning worship service, nor would they spontaneously choose to go to a church after seeing a pithy statement on its marquee. Also, some Sunday faithful would not want to invite a friend to their church because of weak preaching or a frigid atmosphere. Therefore, a halfway house, so to speak, is needed for the not-yet-Christian. There needs to be a place for people to meet Christians and study God's Word without having to attend Sunday worship—where they may be discouraged, intimidated, or feel out of place.

The basic meaning of "post-Christian," simply put, is *after* Christianity. It means that Christianity is no longer the main influence in society. I will not go into all the things that cause a culture to be post-Christian, but a general description of this worldview needs to be given. Christians living in such a culture feel under attack. This shift in culture is very real. The influence of Christianity on our culture is not what it once was. As a result, many Americans know about the church, but it has no bearing on how they live their lives. The diminishing value of Christianity is seen as merely the evolving of a country giving equal weight to all religions or to no religion at all. Post-Christians are not necessarily anti-Christian, but rather their attitude is, "We, as a culture, tried it and it didn't work." It seems extremely arrogant to them to think one religion is superior to another.

Past efforts of evangelism were based on mass campaigns and/or revivals held in local churches. These were patterned after a typical Sunday morning worship service, using vocabulary familiar to church attendees. Friends were to be invited to hear a clear gospel presentation. Due to the changing culture, this style of evangelism is, in large part, no longer effective. Millions of Americans, unlike their parents and grandparents, have no connection to the traditional church. They have no understanding of Christian terminology and lingo. If they did attend an evangelistic campaign similar to Billy Graham's, it would be like landing on Mars. The sermon would sound like strange mutterings, filled with words that had little or no meaning to them.

I think of this when I am driving and see messages on signs such as "Jesus Saves," "Ask Jesus into Your Heart," and "Jesus Is Coming Soon." These may speak to lapsed Christians as a way to get them back to church, but post-Christians have no inkling as to what these messages mean. They do not respond by thinking about their spiritual condition. They see Christianity as just one of the many world religions that have been around a long time. Jesus, if he existed at all, was merely a good man in the same class as Buddha, Confucius, and Muhammad. Also, they do not see themselves as sinners, such as murderers and drug dealers. Several years ago I spoke to my son's math tutor about her spiritual condition. She made it clear to me that she was not a sinner because she had never stolen anything or killed anyone. (She was sorry that I saw myself as a sinner.)

In addition, post-Christians find it difficult to comprehend that God could judge them. They work hard, pay their taxes, and give to charities, so why would God judge them? That idea makes no sense to those of the post-Christian culture. It is not the case that these non-believers are burdened by guilt and shame. They have not been taught that people are born with a sin nature, or that they need a Savior. It is just not in their vocabulary.

This is the culture the American church faces. Obviously, Christians must change the way they interact with post-Christians to have any hope of effectively communicating the gospel to them. This change may be difficult, but is necessary. This is where the small group Bible study can serve as a safe place to introduce them to an authentic Christian culture where they are guaranteed a positive experience. However, in order to provide such an atmosphere, the discipleship group will have to evolve, or be reprogrammed. Participants in traditional discipleship groups are Christians who already know each other, because they usually attend the same church. They gather weekly, biweekly, or monthly. They meet in apartments, homes, and restaurants. They get together to talk about how life is going, read the Bible, and pray. Discipleship groups allow quick bonds to form since participants all share a love for Christ and forgiveness of sins. These groups provide an atmosphere where people find hope as relationships with one another deepen and become more meaningful.

The post-Christian Bible study is for those who are not yet Christians. It is for those who have no relationship to Christ and probably have an agnostic view of the organized church. The initiative for starting this small group originates from a core group of Christians already heavily committed to a discipleship group. They choose, however, for a short period of time to start and lead a Bible study for post-Christians. To do so, however, they will have to leave behind much of what they experienced in the discipleship group. This core group of leaders realizes that the invited participants will be those needing to hear the gospel, not committed Christians. Invited guests will have completely different needs than those in discipleship groups. Post-Christians will not be interested in the deeper requirements of spiritual formation, but they will have questions dealing with the most fundamental questions of faith.

> Matthew 28:19–20
>
> Therefore go and make disciples of all nations, baptizing them in the name of the Father and of the Son and of the Holy Spirit, and teaching them to obey everything I have commanded you. And surely I am with you always, to the very end of the age.

Leaders of the post-Christian Bible study must take the "go" in the Great Commission seriously. Since participants will not come from a discipleship group or from church, leaders realize they have to "go" to potential guests and personally invite them.

Leaders realize that they will not be attending this Bible study for their own spiritual growth. They are meeting for a few weeks to meet the needs of others; those who may never have heard the gospel. For a short period of time, these leaders from a discipleship group seek to serve those without gospel knowledge. What they bring from their discipleship group is commitment to Christ and his Word, and love for those who do not know him. They also bring the assurance that their action is supported with much prayer from their brothers and sisters in the discipleship group.

So, let's summarize the differences between the post-Christian Bible study and the discipleship group Bible study:

1. Goal: "going" instead of "gathering"

2. Composition: post-Christians instead of committed Christians

3. Theme: leading to faith instead of deepening faith

4. Style: The leader is not there to lecture the participants or instruct them in matters of faith. He/she is there to facilitate an atmosphere where people stemming from the post-Christian culture can critique the key elements of the gospel. The leader must insure that each guest feels accepted and feels free to express their opinion. The leader understands that guests may have no knowledge of the Bible. Post-Christian Bible studies are not places where Christians would normally feel comfortable, unless they have been prepared. They are not a place for a deepening of faith. They are not evangelistic events where a theologian or gifted speaker comes and invited guests are confronted with the gospel. They are not outreaches where invited guests can sit in a comfortable atmosphere and discuss hot topics of the day with Christians. Post-Christian Bible studies are open to those who have questions about Christianity and, with the Bible in hand, can discover for themselves what the Bible says about Jesus and their need to trust him. Their questions and concerns have priority no matter how strange, weird, or kooky they may sound. The next chapter focuses on the

unique character of this type of Bible study and the role the discipleship group plays for its foundation, leadership, and future.

2

Bible Study for the Post-Christian

Discipleship groups are fertile ground for those Christians ready to take the next step in their spiritual growth by founding and leading targeted evangelistic strategies. This is why discipleship groups exist. They exist to continually provide fellowship and Bible knowledge, but they also have a specific goal in mind. It is not enough to say, "We meet to deepen our walk with Christ." What does that mean? Obviously, to the Christian it means following Christ's example and seeking out those who do not know him (Luke 19:10). Jesus' entire ministry was based on the principle that the world needs to be saved (John 3:16). Small groups exist to win others to Christ. They have the luxury of being unencumbered by church bureaucracy and have the ability to quickly plan strategies for reaching non-Christians. If discipleship Bible study groups do not plan and execute specific evangelistic missions, they need to re-evaluate why they meet. Although not every member of these groups must lead an evangelistic Bible study, all must be willing to support such a study with prayer and by inviting non-Christians to attend. Discipleship group members who desire to start an outreach to post-Christians must realize that this type of study has a different function and format. If you took a selfie of a post-Christian Bible study, it might look something like this:

Invited Guests

Participants should be those who do not yet know Christ. They should be people that the leader and coworkers already know. They can be family members, office colleagues, people from the gym, or neighbors. The most important thing is that these people do not know the gospel. This is the whole point of the post-Christian Bible study: reaching people who have not made a decision for Christ. The leadership taking a leave of absence from the discipleship group must know non-Christians. This, however, can be a real problem with those who have been Christians for a long time.

There are two universal principles plaguing today's American church. First, the older a church is, the less emphasis it places on evangelism. Second, the number of non-Christian friends decreases proportionately the longer a person is a Christian. I have been in scores of churches where church members had lost all contact with non-Christians or those who knew non-Christians but had no personal relationship with them. Sometimes Christians find themselves spending the bulk of their time in church activities to the detriment of those who do not attend church. One of the worst things a church can do is to tell a new Christian to cut ties with his or her post-Christian friends, unless those friends are truly detrimental to the new believer's walk with God. Potential leaders and coleaders must ask themselves how many post-Christians they know well enough to invite to a Bible study. If the answer is none, there are ways to change this that will be discussed in chapter 3.

Number of Participants

The number of participants attending is varied. I have led groups with as few as two participants and as many as thirteen. There is no rule dictating the amount of attendees. However, the larger the group, the more leadership is needed. If I were leading a post-Christian group with more than three of four people, I would want another Christian there with me for support. Discipleship groups, on the other hand, normally remain small in number because the intimacy and fellowship decreases as the group grows in size. In some cases when the group reaches a certain number, discipleship groups split and form another group. This is not the case with post-Christian Bible studies, because they are designed to end after reaching a specified number of meetings. If attendees desire, the group can continue on with a similar format.

Leadership

Logically, only one person should lead the post-Christian group. The leader must have at least a rudimentary knowledge of the Bible. He/she must believe the Bible is inspired by God (2 Timothy 3:16) and holds the answers to all the basic questions of life (Matthew 4:4; John 6:63). However, if you cannot name all the books of the Bible and quote important Scripture, you are not disqualified from leading a group. If you love Jesus, can find the Table of Contents, and look up chapters and verses, then you are quite capable of leading such a group. Most importantly, the leader must be filled with or controlled by the Holy Spirit (Ephesians 5:18). Leading an evangelistic Bible study is doing God's work, and it must be done in God's way. The Bible is a Spirit-filled text, and it only makes sense that you too are Spirit-filled. In addition, a post-Christian Bible study is seeking to invade Satan's territory. The leader must know this from the outset. This is not a discipleship group where each person is a child of God and is aware of the power of the devil (1 Peter 5:8). The leader is invading Satan's territory and needs the discipleship group's prayer support for protection and wisdom in doing just that.

Post-Christian Bible Study Coworkers

The leader should have, depending upon the number of attendees, two or three others from the discipleship group to provide support during the Bible study. They must also have the same qualities that the leader possesses. Coworkers not only lend support, but also are the ones who invite potential participants. Coworkers will be essential for the future of the small group. In most cases, the guests will want to keep meeting, so there have to be those willing to carry on the work. If the leader prefers to return to his or her discipleship group, or start another group for post-Christians, the coworkers take up the task of forging a new direction for the original group. Never lead a Bible study without coworkers who are willing and able to be taught by example. Having coworkers serves three important functions:

1. They provide help to the leader.
2. They invite guests.
3. They learn how to lead the Bible study themselves.Even if every invited guest makes a decision for Christ, they are still not ready for a discipleship group. The problems post-Christians encounter visiting a church service also hold true for when they join discipleship groups. They would be uncomfortable in that type group for the same reasons they would not feel comfortable in church. So, the Bible study should continue using much the same format as before. In fact, this style of study may be needed for a long time in order to insure the comfort level for the attendees. Most post-Christians need plenty of informal time where they can ask the most basic questions before going into more traditional avenues for spiritual growth.

Places to Meet

Meetings should take place wherever the invited guests would feel comfortable being able to talk and voice their questions and opinions without fear of interruptions or intimidation. If, on a scale of one to ten, with one being the worst place to meet and ten being the best, then the pastor's home would be one and the leader's home or apartment would be ten. A coleader's home is also desirable. Avoid meeting in the church facility because this could inhibit some of the guests from expressing their feelings or lead to the assumption that the group is a church function of some sort.

Regularity of Meetings

Post-Christian Bible studies should meet weekly. However, if this is not possible, then suggest getting together every other week. Too much time between studies leads to a loss of continuity and focus. It also allows time for more things to interfere with the attendees' regular participation. Remember, the meetings are for serving the needs of the invited guests. They should feel the meetings are important, but also know that the schedule is convenient for them.

Number of Meetings

It is crucial to decide on an exact number of times the Bible study will meet. This insures that those invited know that the study has a clear beginning and a specific end. Post-Christians do not like long-term commitment; knowing that the series of meetings has a definite stopping point will encourage their desire to participate. This will also ensure that the leader and coleaders can return to their discipleship group after the last meeting, if they so choose.

The perfect scenario would be meeting once a week for six to eight weeks. This would allow time for the guests to become acquainted with one another and for leaders to easily accomplish the goals of the study. However, this many meetings may not be possible. Four to five meetings are usually the amount of time post-Christians are willing to give for a Bible study.

Leaders will have to adjust how the studies develop depending on the number of times the participants are willing to come, and make sure the study meets the required goal. The goal, of course, is that the guests make a decision for Christ. A person may decide to trust Christ, or they may not. However, the gospel always includes a decision, one way or the other. If the decision is not to trust Christ at that time, this does not prevent them from wanting to continue meeting in this type of setting. Since the leaders have control over the direction of the Bible studies, having this goal in mind, they can dictate how each meeting facilitates reaching for that goal. The key to this is choosing appropriate biblical texts and asking questions that lead to the explanation of the gospel. More will be said about this later.

Refreshments

Refreshments are an absolute necessity. Depending on the time of day, appropriate snacks and drinks should be offered at each meeting. Be creative and offer different coffees from around the world, or pastries from different bakeries in the area. Another idea is to have various teas or fruit drinks from around the world, if available in your area. Use your imagination to come up with foods that will make each meeting a little different. Remember that food items need to be things that are easily consumed while talking and holding a Bible in your lap.

Praying and Singing

I would avoid praying and singing. Remember, participants are not Christians, and praying might make them feel uneasy. Naturally, leaders should pray before and between the meetings, but not at the meetings. Singing would be fine for an icebreaker, if one of the leaders can play a popular secular song on the guitar, as long as it does not distract from the discussion of the Bible. Praying and singing hymns is for discipleship groups, but not a good idea for post-Christian Bible studies.

Follow-Up Activity

Planning a fun activity at the end of the last Bible study is a good way to close out the series. This will facilitate the bonding of the group and encourage additional Bible studies or informal meetings. The activity can be anything that the leaders think would leave a positive feeling for the group and encourage them to bring their families or friends. It could be as simple as a grill party or seeing a movie, to the more extreme activities of paintball or laser tag. Such a follow-up activity communicates to the attendees that they are loved and appreciated as individuals and not evangelistic targets.

Content of the First Meeting

The first meeting sets the tone for the rest of the Bible study, so in many ways it is the most important meeting. Make sure refreshments are available while everyone introduces himself or herself. At this juncture, rather than simply have everyone say their name and something about themselves, it is important to use a creative icebreaker to help with the introductions. Ask guests, using pencil and paper, to sketch a drawing that typifies themselves or their families. Attendees usually draw themselves working out, skiing, or showing the family in a typical activity that exemplifies them. This gets everyone talking and discussing likes and dislikes right away. Then ask each guest what he or she expects from the Bible studies. It is at this point that the leader explains the purpose of the Bible study. Here are two examples of such an explanation:

> *Example 1:* "In the next few weeks we are meeting together to discover the central message of the Bible. We want to use the Bible and determine if it still speaks to us today. If you do not think the Bible is God's Word that is not a problem. But, for the next few weeks, we want to see what the Bible actually says before we criticize it. So, only for the purpose of our discussions, we want to deal with the Bible as though it is God's Word. The only

rules we have are: everyone joins in the discussion, and no question is dumb."

Example 2: "We are meeting together in order to discover for ourselves what the Bible has to say to us. We want to do this by looking at some specific parts of the Bible, asking questions about them, and discussing whether they have anything to say specifically about our lives. We want to study these portions of the Bible and take them seriously instead of arguing whether they are true or not. We want to be open to what the text says before we criticize it."

These explanations show the reason for the meetings and let those who may be antagonistic toward the Bible feel comfortable and not pressured. It promotes discussion and harmony rather than constantly arguing whether the Bible is God's word or not. It may become necessary to remind the group of these reasons as time passes. I have found this explanation satisfies those who do not believe in the authority of the Bible. It is very important that guests understand they are free to express their opinions and ask any questions they may have without fear of ridicule or judgment.

The leader then acquaints the guests with the Bible. The leader should provide the Bibles because it is important that everyone uses the *same translation*. This makes discussing specific biblical texts easier. Also, use a translation that is easy to understand. Remember, invited guests may never have held a Bible in their hands and need a translation that they can easily comprehend. There are many good modern translations available, so choose one that post-Christians easily understand. Bibles can be expensive, so those in the discipleship group can be asked to pitch in to help purchase them. Smartphones and tablets are great for personal Bible reading and study, however, it is best to use books so that everyone is literally on the same page. It will also minimize possible distractions in the group.

Because post-Christians may have never been exposed to the Bible, the leader needs to mention that the Bible is divided into the Old and New Testaments. Show where the Table of Contents is found and point out any maps included at the back to find places mentioned in the Bible. You might also want to mention that paragraph breaks and section titles are not part of the Bible, but are aids to the reader. Turn to the Table of Contents, where guests can actually see how the Bible is divided into two major portions. Find the Gospel of Mark, for example, in the Table of Contents. Point out the page number where it starts, and then have them turn to the book. It is a good idea to also do this with a book in the Old Testament. The leader should *always use the Table of Contents and give the page number(s)* when referring to a specific text. Explain how the chapters and verses are numbered for easy and speedy detection. Point out where the chapter and verse numbers are located. Although this may seem elementary, it insures that guests never feel foolish or embarrassed while searching for a verse in the Bible. It is important that the coworkers also use the Table of Contents when finding Bible passages. This helps make sure that attendees feel comfortable using the Bible for themselves and is another way of showing your respect and love for the participants.

The remaining time is given to questions and discussion of the chosen passage for the evening. Remember, the chosen passage needs to be one that speaks to the needs of the readers. This passage should be a text that plainly points to the central message of the Bible, and leads to great discussion or questions. I always use John 3:16. In chapter 5 I will explain why I use this verse.

Make sure the Bibles stay with the leaders. This insures that a Bible is not lost or forgotten for the next meeting. If an attendee asks to take a Bible home, they most certainly can do so. When this happens, be sure to give him or her a call before the next meeting and remind them to not to forget to bring it. Before the guests leave, remind them of the time and place for the next meeting. Remember, as hard as it may be, do not end in prayer. The time for that is after the guests leave, when the leader and coleader(s) pray together for the group.

Normal Timeframe for the Bible Study

It is important for the guests to know that the discussion group meeting has a clear start and specific end. Although an atmosphere of informality should be maintained, the guests need to know they are free to leave at a certain time.

Small talk/chitchat	10 minutes
Bible discussion/study	45–60 minutes
Further one-on one discussion	30 minutes
Total	1.5–2 hours

It is important that the study ends at least twenty to thirty minutes before the official close. If the meeting ends at 10:00, end the study around 9:30. The reason for this is interesting: the best, and most personal, discussions occur *after* the end of the Bible study. I cannot explain this phenomenon, but it is one I have observed over and over again. The leader and coworkers need to keep a close watch on the clock so that this valuable time at the end is not cut short.

3

Inviting Participants

Who Do You Invite?

If you wonder who to invite, the answer is that you should invite people you already know and with whom you have a good relationship. Potential guests must know you well enough to trust you and must feel comfortable enough around you to know you would never do anything to embarrass them or put them on the spot. You invite post-Christians you know from the office, the fitness center, from your child's soccer game, or any other social setting. Statistics show that 70–90 percent of Christians came to faith because of personal acquaintances, close friends, and relatives. Rarely do people come to faith because of evangelistic outreaches, such as home visitations or special events at church. This is where your discipleship group can be helpful. Ask those in your group how many non-Christians they know and how close they are to them. If two or three in your group have close relationships with post-Christians, ask them to be your coworkers. They in turn will invite those they already know to come to the post-Christian Bible discussion group. Take a look at the diagram below and fill in your name at the center. Think about all the people you know from all areas of your life. Write down the names of those who you think might respond to your invitation to a Bible discussion group.

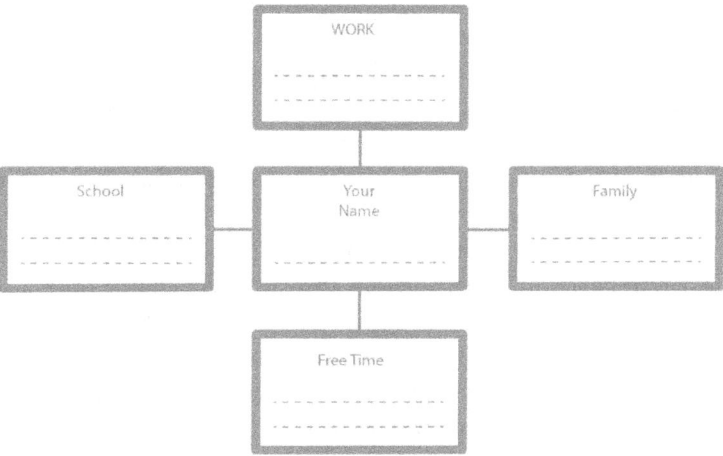

How Do You Invite?

When you invite the people you know, make sure that you are upfront about what the discussion group entails. Tell them that you want to get together five or six times to discuss the Bible and see if it has any relevance for today. No surprises! Invite people the same way you would invite them to your birthday party. Be honest and natural. Always email or call those whom you have *personally* invited a few days before the meeting, as a reminder. One woman invited thirteen women she knew from her neighborhood to meet in her home. A few days before the first meeting, she mailed out cards that, when opened, took the form of a house, with the reminder inside. This showed how important the Bible discussion group was to this woman and really impressed the guests. Everyone came and never missed a meeting. She had, of course, her own discipleship group backing her up with prayer and ideas.

As mentioned before, there are many times when Christians have no close relationship with post-Christians. There is a remedy for that, but it will take some extra prayer and planning. Or, you may find that you know some unchurched people, but your relationship is such that you do not yet feel comfortable inviting them to an evangelistic Bible discussion group. In both cases, the problem can be eliminated, but not without a radical change in how evangelism is understood. Personal relationships are the key to reaching post-Christians and ensuring that they become disciples of Christ. Statistics show that personal relationships not only lead to conversions, but new converts are more likely to attend church, and continue attending, when a friend or family member leads them to Christ.

American Christians must change their expectations of evangelism in post-Christian America. Instead of depending on evangelistic events at church, TV preachers, or other professionals to win people to Christ, Christians should concentrate on building relationships. We must learn to listen to post-Christians instead of giving them pat answers. Each human being has a basic need to be encouraged, valued, and understood. Healthy relationships with post-Christians begin with discovering what their life goals are and what things are important to them. Christians should make it their mission to invest time in the lives of non-Christians. At this point, take a moment to reflect on how much time you invest in the lives of post-Christians.

Time With Non-Christians

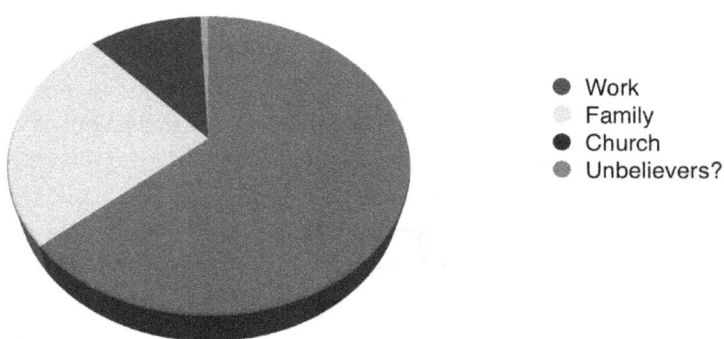

Christians have only so much time to give. There are parts of one's life that cannot be shortchanged or avoided. However, there are things that can be changed, depending upon priorities. The church exists as a witness to those without Christ, and we attend church to give us wisdom and strength to carry out this mission. If evangelism is a priority, then Christians have to make time to be with non-Christians. It reminds me of the apocryphal tale of the Seamen's Rescue Society. The story goes that the Rescue Society was a crack rescue team. They spent hours and hours training for rescue. However, even after logging thousands of hours training, they never actually rescued any shipwrecked sailors. This describes many Christians, spending their entire lives being equipped and logging thousands of hours in discipleship groups, but never really helping introduce anyone to Christ.

Filling the Pond

I grew up on a ranch in East Texas, where there are many ponds from which cattle can drink. During a drought some of the ponds dry up, causing all the fish to die. As a result, even when they are full of water there are no fish in the ponds. You can use the juiciest worms and fish as long as you desire, but you will never catch a fish because there are none. Some discipleship groups and churches experience a similar problem. Jesus called us to "fish for people," (Matthew 4:19), but with so little time available for non-Christians, there are no fish in our pond to catch. How does a church get fish into its pond? How do Christians build deeper relationships with non-Christians, reaching the point where they can invite them to a post-Christian Bible discussion group?

One church in Germany, founded using evangelistic home Bible discussion groups, realized its pond was running low on fish. The members needed to develop new relationships and/or deepen the ones they already had. They solved their empty pond problem by deciding to retool their traditional annual church retreat, where the church went for an entire weekend to a beautiful nearby forest to pray and worship God. The church believed that a similar retreat could be used to reach those not attending church, so they came up with the idea of a "church retreat without church." This meant that the retreat would follow the basic rule of the evangelistic Bible discussions: plan an event solely dedicated to meeting the needs of not-yet-Christians. These retreats would be molded to fit the cultural needs of, in this case, post-Christian men. The response has been so positive that this church has made these retreats an ongoing, much anticipated experience for twenty years now. Their pond is continually being restocked!

Just as the discipleship group is the launching point for the post-Christian Bible discussion group, the church retreat can become the launching point for acquiring or strengthening bonds with the unchurched. Just as the discipleship group must branch into a very different form in order to evangelize post-Christians, the church retreat can evolve into a culturally friendly form for non-Christians to build relationships to a point where they will come to a discussion group. Just as leaders of evangelistic Bible discussion groups must discard most of the forms found in other church groups, leaders of non-Christian oriented church retreats will need to retool some activities. There are prayers before each meal, but beyond that, there is nothing resembling the traditional church retreat—no sermons, no devotions, no Bible studies, and no worship songs. This retreat is for the purpose of getting to know those without Christ. Non-Christians must first become acquainted with Christians before the gospel will have any meaning to them. Relationships take time to develop. It may take years for people to feel comfortable enough to join a Bible discussion group, but this is a reality that American Christians must recognize.

In a post-Christian culture, it takes an average of eight years for a person to come to faith after initial contact with the gospel. Think about this: Even in a Christian culture a person rarely believes the gospel the first time he or she hears it. The gospel must be heard many times and in different venues before a decision is made. Now, consider a person who has had little or no contact with Christians, has a warped view of the church, and is an agnostic. In addition, the entire culture has an aversion to Christianity. It is little wonder then that it takes a long time for a post-Christian to trust Christ or fully comprehend the Bible's message. This is

Inviting Participants

difficult for many American Christians to believe. I was attacked as a heretic in one American church when I explained how long it took for someone to become a Christian in Europe. These folks believed that the Holy Spirit immediately opens the heart of a person to a living faith, without them ever having any contact with Christians or previously hearing the gospel. This can happen and does happen; however, these cases are exceptions—not the rule.

During the rather heated discussion at this church, one person claimed he had spontaneously trusted Christ in his car while listening to gospel radio. However, after being pressed, he admitted he had previously attended church and had heard the gospel before his conversion. Can a person who has never heard the gospel or met a Christian miraculously come to faith? Absolutely. However, one would have to really twist the Great Commission and ignore the normal practices in the Book of Acts to believe that this is always the will of God.

This is dramatically displayed in John 4, where many in the village of Sychar were converted. Jesus says that the disciples had the "easy work" of harvesting souls. However, he emphasizes that others who had previously visited the village had done the "hard work" of preparing the harvest:

John 4:37-38

Thus the saying "One sows and another reaps" is true. I sent you to reap what you have not worked for. Others have done the hard work, and you have reaped the benefits of their labor.

Jesus makes it clear that the most difficult task is preparing people to hear the gospel. The person who actually leads a person to Christ has the easy job, and has no room to brag about their evangelistic skills!

There are cases in Acts where people are converted through a miracle, such as the fortuneteller and the Philippian jailer in Acts 16. Both of these conversions appear to be both spontaneous and miraculous. However, most conversions resulted from those who already had some contact with the Scriptures or with believers

(Acts 8; 10; 16:13–15). It was also the usual practice of the missionaries in Acts first to visit municipal synagogues, just as Jesus had done (Matthew 9:35; Acts 13:4–5; 14:1; 17:1–4).

Summary

Who do you invite?

1. Invite people from work.
2. Invite people from school or college.
3. Invite family members.
4. Invite people from your free time activities.
5. Invite other parents you know.

How do you invite them?

1. Invite them personally.
2. Do not con them. Tell them exactly what the discussion group entails.
3. Be sure to communicate the commitment level—the number of meetings.
4. A short time before the first meeting, remind them.

How do you build relationships with post-Christians?

1. Stress getting to know them—not evangelistic events.
2. Love people instead of lecturing them.
3. Encourage post-Christians by listening to them.
4. Be willing to give time to them.

What if you know no post-Christians to invite?

1. Plan a "church retreat without church."
2. Plan an outing or activity that meets post-Christians' needs.
3. Keep the long view, the "hard work," in mind.

What do Post-Christians want?

1. They want to hear *what you know, after they know* you are interested in them.
2. Show concern and understanding. Their lives may be a mess.
3. Get to know their world before you talk about your world.
4. Use language they understand.
5. Have a little humor. If they become a Christian, they want to enjoy it, not just bear it.
6. Do not talk about your church all the time. It probably has no meaning to them anyway. It is also possible they have a negative view of church.
7. Do not just talk about your faith; instead, show it by how much you care about others.
8. Give them time! Do not try to explain everything all at once or expect a quick conversion. Let them know that God is willing to take time and work with them.
9. Tell them how God can make a difference in their daily life: their character, their family, and their relationships. They want to know that God is God outside of Sunday.
10. Show them how they can get to know Jesus from the Bible. Let them know they can get to know him personally by reading his Word.

4

The Role of the Discussion Group Leader

It is not the duty of the post-Christian Bible discussion leader to lecture or teach the guests. It is not his or her job to correct answers, or add commentary. The leader does not preach sermons or dominate the discussion in any way. It is the leader's duty to guide the discussion with appropriate, thought-provoking questions and to summarize the discussion from time to time. The leader is to keep the group on course toward the intended goal and to make sure that everyone gets a chance to voice his or her opinion. Most importantly, the leader and coworkers are, as much as possible, to keep opinions to themselves. Leaders guide the discussion with questions and short summaries to insure that guests stay on the topic and are able to express their opinions and comments; the views of the leaders are not the focus.

The Role of the Discussion Group Leader

The Golden Rules of the Group Leader

1. Keep the discussion moving. Keep it from stalling by restating questions or comments. This also insures that the entire group understands them.
2. Make sure that participants do not get too far off of the current discussion.
3. Keep personal opinions private unless or until you are asked what you believe. This helps keep the leader from talking too much, which is a temptation in most groups.
4. Pay attention so as to make sure that everyone gets a chance to talk. Do not let only one or two people dominate the discussion.
5. Be patient and allow time for the guests to answer questions.
6. Develop an atmosphere of love, acceptance, and tolerance. Encourage those holding back to express their viewpoints by reacting positively when they do speak.
7. Respect differences of opinions. When possible, let the group answer questions and make comments, rather than the leader.
8. Summarize the group's comments, especially at the end of the meeting. The leader can make or break the goal of Bible discussion group. In general, group leaders tend to talk too much. We Christians are prone to correct false teachings or wrong conclusions in order to make sure no one is misled or misinformed. However, if the leader corrects false notions or comments every time someone's opinion contradicts the Bible, the group discussion is dead. Attendees will not want to say what they really think, and that is disastrous for the discussion. If the leader and coworkers cannot control their desire to interject themselves, then they will never learn what the guests know and what they believe. It is through freedom of thought and expression that the leader and coworkers discover where the guests are spiritually. Some

guests actually may be seeking truth; others may be confused; some may be antagonistic toward anything spiritual. The leader needs to know where each group member is coming from in order to plan what texts should be used for the coming meetings and exactly how to guide the discussions toward the gospel message. These things become evident if the leaders are able to be quiet and let the guests say what they think. Remember, the goal is not just to become knowledgeable of the Bible or the Christian faith in general, but rather that people come to faith in Christ.

This style of leading a Bible discussion group for post-Christians is diametrically opposed to the way of leading a discipleship group. Discipleship groups are where false doctrine and wrong notions about the Christian faith are dealt with and corrected. The discipleship group leader is quick to insert corrective comments if someone seems to be straying toward a cult, sect, or bad theology. The role of the discipleship group leader is to point out the dangers of false interpretations and guard the group against views contrary to the Scriptures. The post-Christian discussion leader and coleaders want false views and beliefs to surface so that appropriate Bible verses can be used in upcoming sessions. It is the job of these group leaders to allow the Bible to answer questions and let it correct false doctrine. More will be said about this in the next chapter.

In summary, the role of the leader in a post-Christian Bible discussion group is:

1. Direct—do not preach.
2. Summarize comments and follow up with a question when the discussion stalls.
3. Avoid correcting or commenting on every false statement.
4. Allow the Bible to speak for you.
5. Listen . . . silence is golden.

The Role of the Discussion Group Leader

Dealing with Discussion Group Problems

No matter how much the leader prepares or how he or she conducts the meetings, there will be challenges from time to time. What do you do when problems arise? The following are common challenges and suggestions in dealing with them:

1. Someone talks non-stop. The best way to deal with such a person is to interrupt them when they take a breath, briefly summarize what they have said, and quickly ask another person to give their opinion.

2. Someone gives a completely false answer to a question. Repeat the question to make sure the person has correctly understood it. If the person sticks with the fully false answer, let it stand and ask someone else his or her opinion.

3. No one speaks after you ask a question. When this happens, simply call on someone to answer the question. If no one answers, then you go ahead and answer it and then ask the group what they think of your answer. If there is still no response, this is when your coworker(s) can offer a comment or answer the question. Coworkers are there to help out during such times when the discussion hits a wall. The leader and coworkers should plan ahead for when they can help bridge gaps in the discussion.

4. Discussion gets off the subject. This is a frequent occurrence. When it happens, simply say that the group needs to get back to the topic. If appropriate, the leader can offer to cover the new issue on another evening. You can also summarize what is being discussed, and then ask a question related to the topic for the evening.

5. Guests disagree. This does not happen often, but if it does, identify the area of contention and suggest that the Bible be used to resolve the question in dispute. If the leader cannot immediately suggest a passage, simply say that the question will be answered at the next meeting. It is impossible to always have a Bible passage in mind that answers every

question. Postponing the discussion on a particular topic alleviates pressure on the leader to spontaneously answer every question.

6. Someone never talks. This can occur as a result of certain individuals dominating the meeting, such as the non-stop talker. If this happens, ask the silent person his or her opinion on the topic. This may be necessary throughout the meetings because some people need to be encouraged to talk. If their personality is one that results in their not wanting to talk, respect this. However, occasionally ask their opinion so they do not feel left out and so the leader can discover what they think.

7. Cult members show up. I do not know how they know when a new Bible study starts, but Mormons or Jehovah's Witnesses will occasionally show up. If this happens, find out after the meeting if they are sincerely seeking the truth. If they only want to spread false doctrine, tell them kindly not to return.

The Importance of the Icebreaker

The Bible discussion group leader should always open the meeting with an icebreaker or "hook." This sets the tone for the meeting and helps avoid some of the previously mentioned problems. Guests come to the meeting with the workday behind them, maybe a bad one. Perhaps they just had a quarrel with their spouse, child, other relative, friend, or coworker. They arrive with all kinds of concerns and worries, with the last thing on their mind being a Bible verse. The hook should be a fun activity that everyone can identify with. For the first meeting it needs to be something that introduces each attendee to one another in a light-hearted way. At each meeting it should be something that not only gets the guests relaxed, but also introduces the chosen Bible passage for the evening. The following are examples of Bible passages with possible icebreakers:

The Role of the Discussion Group Leader

Chosen passage: John 3:16—God's greatest gift

Icebreaker: Gifts are something that can expose a person's likes and dislikes; what he/she feels is important or unimportant. Ask guests to answer one or all of the following questions:
1. What is the greatest gift you have ever received?
2. What is the greatest gift you have ever given someone?
3. When someone gives me something, I feel _____.
4. When I give someone a beautiful gift, I feel _____. These questions lead to a great discussion and serve to introduce the greatest gift God gave to the world—Jesus Christ.

Chosen passage: 2 Peter 3:9—What is important to God?

Icebreaker: What is important to people? What do they feel is a necessity? Ask guests to imagine they are marooned on a deserted island. From the list below, they are allowed to choose three things they would want with them.
1. Golf club with balls
2. Gun with ammunition
3. Box full of novels
4. Jeep full of gas
5. Bible
6. Survival book
7. Surfboard
8. TV with batteries and solar panel
9. First aid kit
10. Playing cards
11. Cell phone

12. Batteries for the cell phone.

Icebreakers are essential elements that should be developed. The last thing a leader wants is for the meetings to be boring. Use your imagination to think up good icebreakers that spark the interest of the guests. A great resource for good questions and icebreakers is the *Serendipity Study Bible*. It is loaded with great ideas for questions and offers all kinds of helps for the discussion group leader. Amazon has a large selection of books on icebreakers for small groups. Another resource is your youth pastor. He or she will no doubt have resource material for icebreakers and hooks for the youth group. These can be easily reprogrammed for the Bible discussion group.

5

Developing Good Questions

Assume that you have enlisted two coworkers from your discipleship group and have invited five people to a series of five Bible discussions, meeting two hours every Thursday evening from 7:30 to 9:30. The coworkers have been trained according to the principles found in chapter 4, and your discipleship group knows of the meetings so they will be backing you up with prayer and encouragement.

As mentioned in chapter 2, you explain the purpose of the group and state the ground rules at the first meeting. You also start the Bible discussion with an appropriate text. I mentioned that I always use John 3:16 as the first text to begin a discussion because this verse evokes one or all of the three questions post-Christians always ask. These three questions will eventually come up and I choose to deal with them at the beginning. The three questions are:
1. If God loves the world, why is there so much evil?
2. What about those who have never heard of Jesus?
3. What about Muslims, Buddhists, and Hindus?I have never led a discussion group where these three questions were not asked at some point. These are serious questions that must be answered and the issue is how to answer them. You may feel unqualified to

delve into any of these important issues facing post-Christians, but the Bible answers these questions and there is no need to give your own viewpoint, theology, or philosophy. Find the text(s) that answer(s) the specific question(s) and allow the Bible to speak for itself. This may be a difficult principle to grasp, and even more difficult to practice. However, I believe God speaks to the heart of non-Christians through the Scriptures.

The Role of the Holy Spirit

John 16:7–11

But I tell you the truth: It is good for you that I am going away. Unless I go away, the Counselor will not come to you; but if I go, I will send him to you. When he comes, he will convict the world of guilt in regard to sin and righteousness and judgment: in regard to sin, because men do not believe in me; in regard to righteousness, because I am going to the Father, where you can see me no longer; and in regard to judgment, because the Prince of this word now stands condemned.

We should memorize this passage for two reasons. First, it shows the prominence of the role of the Holy Spirit, the Counselor, in dealing with those in need of salvation. There is no greater person that can convict people of their need for salvation other than the Holy Spirit. Second, it explains the nature of the problem of the post-Christian. The post-Christian is not someone who needs help solving personal problems, but rather someone who needs a Savior and freedom through Jesus Christ from the domination of Satan.

This is paramount in understanding the role of the group leader, whose job is guiding the post-Christian to the Bible texts revealing their sinfulness and need for Jesus. It is not the leader's job to help the group gain a better understanding of the Bible or learn interesting insights from Scripture. That may occur in the process, but it is not the task or goal of the leader. The goal is to help those in the group in their understanding that as sinners they are under the judgment of God. As already stated, post-Christians do not see themselves as sinners, and there is little chance of our convincing them otherwise. However, it is the role of the Holy Spirit to do what no human agent can do: convict of sin, righteousness, and judgment.

> 2 Timothy 3:16–17
>
> All Scripture is God-breathed and is useful for teaching, rebuking, correcting and training in righteousness, so that the man of God may be thoroughly equipped for every good work.

> Hebrews 4:12–13
>
> The word of God is living and active. Sharper than any double-edged sword, it penetrates even to dividing soul and spirit, joints and marrow; it judges the thoughts and attitudes of the heart. Nothing in all creation is hidden from God's sight. Everything is uncovered and laid bare before the eyes of him to whom we must give account.

The Holy Spirit works through the inspired text. He can convince of the truth when humans cannot. We may not be accustomed to this type of dialogue—letting God speak through the Bible text to the heart of the non-Christian without our own commentary—however, we must let him work this way.

Developing Questions to Facilitate Discussions

Asking good questions is a powerful tool in opening post-Christians' eyes to ideas with which they might otherwise disagree. These questions often lead to a sincere search for the truth. I call this the D.U.A. Method: *Discovery—Understanding—Application*. John 3:16 is used as our sample text, along with suggested questions.

> For God so loved the world that he gave his one and only Son, that whoever believes in him shall not perish but have eternal life.

1. *Discovery Questions*: The goal of discovery questions is to discover basic components of the passage. These questions are answered from simple observation of what is stated in the passage. What was said or done? What is it talking about?
2. *Understanding Questions*: The goal of understanding questions is to dig deeper into the passage. These questions deal with interpreting what the verse is saying and, usually, they are not answered directly from the text. What does "the world" mean? Who is "his one and only Son" referring to? What is eternal life? Who is speaking?
3. *Application Questions*: The goal of application questions is to discover how to put the truths of the text into practice. This helps reach our intended goal of evangelism. What is this text asking us to believe? What attitudes and/or behaviors need to be changed? Does any action need to be taken? The D.U.A. Method can be used for any text, with the leader preparing questions in advance for the discussion group. Advance planning involves anticipating what questions could be asked. Good questions are the way the discussion group leader guides the discussion and keeps it from stalling or getting off track. It is important that the leader becomes familiar with the entire paragraph or context of the passage, in this case John 3:16. During the discussion, guests will often read the surrounding verses on their own out of curiosity. This can lead to some interesting questions. Someone once asked me the meaning of John 3:14.

> And as Moses lifted up the serpent in the wilderness even so must the Son of man be lifted up.

What in the world did this verse mean? What did Moses and a snake have to do with Jesus? I panicked, asking what the others thought about the verse. I then said that it was a good question and that I would discuss it at the next meeting. This is how the leader

Developing Good Questions

can postpone going into unfamiliar theological territory. It gives the leader and coworkers time to find a passage dealing with the question. So, there is no need to be fearful of having to answer a tough question; simply put it off until the next meeting!

At the next meeting, we read Numbers 21:4–9, which is the passage referred to in John 3:14.

> They traveled from Mount Hor along the route to the Red Sea, to go around Edom. But the people grew impatient on the way; they spoke against God and against Moses, and said, "Why have you brought us up out of Egypt to die in the wilderness? There is no bread! There is no water! And we detest this miserable food!"
>
> Then the Lord sent venomous snakes among them; they bit the people and many Israelites died. The people came to Moses and said, "We sinned when we spoke against the Lord and against you. Pray that the Lord will take the snakes away from us." So Moses prayed for the people. The Lord said to Moses, "Make a snake and put it up on a pole; anyone who is bitten can look at it and live." So Moses made a bronze snake and put it up on a pole. Then when anyone was bitten by a snake and looked at the bronze snake, he lived.

1. *Discovery Questions*: What is the text talking about? Who are the main characters?
2. *Understanding Questions*: Why were the people angry? Who were they angry with? Why did God punish the people? How did the people sin?
3. *Application Questions*: Would you have looked at the snake? Why would someone refuse to look at the snake? What does this text have to do with Jesus? As we discussed the passage, it came out how crazy it seemed that the Israelites had to look upon the object that was causing their demise. This is how some felt and refused to do as Moses commanded. It made no sense to them. Others put aside their pride and

looked upon the snake in faith and lived. This directly tied into faith in Christ. It may seem ridiculous that the crucifixion of a relatively unknown Jewish carpenter saves us from our sins, but, nevertheless, this is the essence of faith. We do not have to understand everything to exercise faith.

I realized that God used this question to reveal more about how true faith is exercised. The group had to wrestle with what the Bible said about the serpent and not with my explanation. God really does use his Word to speak to people. We must learn to trust Scripture more and not our own explanations. This lets us off the hook because guests have to argue directly with what God says. We can remind them that it is not what we are saying but rather what the Bible says. We can also remind them that we have all agreed for the sake of these meetings to treat the Bible as though it is God's Word. Yes, there may be times when the leader has to interject an explanation, but these must be kept to a minimum.

This bears repeating. Refrain from directly answering a question. Instead ask yourself: How does the Bible answer this question? This brings a new dynamic for the leader. He or she is not under pressure to come up with pat philosophical or theological answers. The leader uses the Bible to answer questions. The guests then are not arguing with the leader, and they have to deal with the text. This is the point of the Bible discussion group. Guests are confronted with what the Bible says, not the viewpoints of the leader. This is the most important component of leading a discussion. I cannot stress how important this is. Difficult questions are simply deferred until the next meeting. This gives the leader time to find an appropriate text and to develop good questions that promote discussion.

Here is another example using the D.U.A. Method. In this case a longer passage is considered:

> John 4:1–26
>
> The Pharisees heard that Jesus was gaining and baptizing more disciples than John, although in fact it was not Jesus who baptized, but his disciples. When the Lord

Developing Good Questions

learned of this, he left Judea and went back once more to Galilee. Now he had to go through Samaria. So he came to a town in Samaria called Sychar, near the plot of ground Jacob had given to his son Joseph. Jacob's well was there, and Jesus, tired as he was from the journey, sat down by the well. It was about the sixth hour. When a Samaritan woman came to draw water, Jesus said to her, "Will you give me a drink?" (His disciples had gone into the town to buy food.) The Samaritan woman said to him, "You are a Jew and I am a Samaritan woman. How can you ask me for a drink?" (For Jews do not associate with Samaritans.) Jesus answered her, "If you knew the gift of God and who it is that asks you for a drink, you would have asked him and he would have given you living water." "Sir," the woman said, "you have nothing to draw with and the well is deep. Where can you get this living water? Are you greater than our father Jacob, who gave us the well and drank from it himself, as did also his sons and his flocks and herds?" Jesus answered, "Everyone who drinks this water will be thirsty again, but whoever drinks the water I give him will never thirst. Indeed, the water I give him will become in him a spring of water welling up to eternal life." The woman said to him, "Sir, give me this water so that I won't get thirsty and have to keep coming here to draw water." He told her, "Go, call your husband and come back." "I have no husband," she replied. Jesus said to her, "You are right when you say you have no husband. The fact is, you have had five husbands, and the man you now have is not your husband. What you have just said is quite true." "Sir," the woman said, "I can see that you are a prophet. Our fathers worshiped on this mountain, but you Jews claim that the place where we must worship is in Jerusalem." Jesus declared, "Believe me, woman, a time is coming when you will worship the Father neither on this mountain nor in Jerusalem. You Samaritans worship what you do not know; we worship what we do know, for salvation is from the Jews. Yet a time is coming and has now come when the true worshipers will worship the Father in spirit and truth, for they are the kind of worshipers the Father seeks. God is spirit, and his worshipers must worship in spirit and in truth." The woman said, "I know that Messiah" (called Christ) "is coming. When he comes, he will explain everything to us." Then Jesus declared, "I who speak to you am he."

1. *Discovery Questions*: What is this text talking about? Who are the main characters? Where did this event take place?
2. *Understanding Questions*: Why was Jesus at the well? Why was the woman there? Why did she think he was a prophet? Why did Jesus "have to go" through Samaria? (At this point the leader could show a map in the back of the Bible showing that Samaria was between Judea and Galilee; Jesus had to go through Samaria to get to Galilee.) What is "eternal life"?
3. *Application Questions*: What does the term "Messiah" mean today? If the Messiah came, what would be your reaction? How would society react to someone claiming to be the Messiah? This passage is important because it shows how Jesus interacted with an individual and he clearly says who he is. He presents himself as the Messiah, the one for whom the woman was waiting. Jesus is interested in individuals, no matter their station in life or how messed up their situation may be. This passage reveals how Jesus loves people regardless of their condition. He shows himself to be graceful and merciful, but he exposes sin for what it is. He makes no excuses for sin, but also is ready to forgive and show mercy. Jesus speaks to individuals today through the Holy Spirit.

The Three Questions

As previously mentioned, there are three questions that will come up during the course of the Bible discussion group meetings, for which the leader can prepare ahead of time. Leaders must choose passages that they feel adequately answer these questions. The following passages are only examples of the many that can be used:

Developing Good Questions

If God loves the world, why is there so much evil?

Passage: Genesis 3:1–19

1. *Discovery Questions*: Who are the main characters in the text? Where did this event take place?
2. *Understanding Questions*: How did Adam and Eve disobey God? Why did they disobey God? Why did they hide from God? How did God punish Adam and Eve?
3. *Application Questions*: How does this text explain evil? Do you feel this gives a good answer or a poor answer as to why there is evil? This passage can lead to a deeper discussion of general and personal sin. This text reveals the original source of all evil and shows what evil is—disobeying God. It will certainly lead to even more questions about the nature of evil and suffering in the world. This will give the leader an opportunity to share other passages dealing with sin and evil. However, this text is foundational for all others.

What about those who have never heard about Jesus?

Passage: Romans 1:18–20

1. *Discovery Questions*: What is this passage referring to? How many times is the word "God" used?
2. *Understanding Questions*: What do you think of when you hear the word "wrath?" How does God reveal himself to mankind? What is "what has been made" referring to?
3. *Application Questions*: What do we know about God from creation? Why does this passage say that no one has an excuse? For what are people without excuse? This passage is a clear example of how the Bible answers the basic issues of human faith and spirituality. It shows that God tries to reach everyone and no one has an excuse for rejecting God. A young woman who was an atheist attended one meeting I led. She was reared in East Germany, had no knowledge

of God or the Bible, and spoke little during the meetings. In fact, at the first meeting she said she did not want to be called on for questions, so I respected her wish. However, while reading this text she spoke up and said, "I am one of those people." I asked her what she meant. She said, "I am one of those people that God is trying to reach." I nearly fell out of my chair. Here was a clear case of the Holy Spirit speaking to the heart of this young woman through the Scriptures. We must understand how powerful the Scriptures are and let the Holy Spirit work through the Bible.

What about the Muslims, Buddhists, and Hindus?

Passage John 10:1–10

1. *Discovery Questions*: Who is speaking? What is he talking about?
2. *Understanding Questions*: What is the passage saying about the nature of sheep? Who do the sheep represent?
3. *Application Questions*: If Jesus met Buddha (563–483 BC) and Confucius (551–479 BC) on the street, what would he say to them? (The leader may mention that both lived hundreds of years before Jesus.) Was Jesus tolerant or intolerant of other religious leaders? The answers I have gotten from the above question are the same: "Jesus would tell Confucius and Buddha that they are thieves and robbers." This is amazing since the people are not Christians, but know what Jesus is saying about himself. Clearly, this passage is not referring to Buddha or Confucius, but to the former Jewish teachers claiming to be the Messiah. However, the intent of the passage is that Jesus separates himself from other religious leaders.

Developing Good Questions

The Power of Scripture

Luke 16:19–31

"There was a rich man who was dressed in purple and fine linen and lived in luxury every day. At his gate was laid a beggar named Lazarus, covered with sores and longing to eat what fell from the rich man's table. Even the dogs came and licked his sores. "The time came when the beggar died and the angels carried him to Abraham's side. The rich man also died and was buried. In hell, where he was in torment, he looked up and saw Abraham far away, with Lazarus by his side. So he called to him, 'Father Abraham, have pity on me and send Lazarus to dip the tip of his finger in water and cool my tongue, because I am in agony in this fire.' "But Abraham replied, 'Son, remember that in your lifetime you received your good things, while Lazarus received bad things, but now he is comforted here and you are in agony. And besides all this, between us and you a great chasm has been fixed, so that those who want to go from here to you cannot, nor can anyone cross over from there to us.' "He answered, 'Then I beg you, father, send Lazarus to my father's house, for I have five brothers. Let him warn them, so that they will not also come to this place of torment.' "Abraham replied, 'They have Moses and the Prophets; let them listen to them.' " 'No, father Abraham,' he said, 'but if someone from the dead goes to them, they will repent.' "He said to him, 'If they do not listen to Moses and the Prophets, they will not be convinced even if someone rises from the dead.'"

This is an amazing statement. Abraham says that if someone does not believe the Bible—in this case the Old Testament—they will not believe even if someone rises from the dead and speaks to them! When post-Christians are confronted with Scripture, there is no greater power that can convince them of the truth. Trust the Bible; it is the best evangelist. This fact gives us confidence and comfort.

The post-Christian Bible discussion group is a great example of how God reaches those who do not know him. In his grace, God has chosen not only to use his Word in evangelism, but also to allow Christians to partner with him. This is where God's people experience real joy and excitement. I have seen angry agnostics' whole countenance and attitude change after a few hours of reading and discussing the Bible. It is truly an amazing thing to witness. Once you have seen this happen, you want to expose more and more post-Christians to God's Word and witness the changing power of Scripture. They have heard the gospel for the first time and have actually read it from the Bible. They may not trust Christ immediately, but they have started their journey to salvation by faith.

6

Explaining Evangelism

Evangelism—communicating the gospel in a way that the hearer understands and responds to it—is the reason for the post-Christian Bible discussion group. The group's goal is that in the last meeting guests are given an opportunity to respond to the gospel. If this is not done, then the whole process means nothing. The mindset of the leaders must be that they are the ones God is using to initially present the gospel to the guests. They should see themselves only as spokes in the wheel of the whole process of evangelism, which may take years. However, they are the most important because they have the privilege of introducing Jesus to the hearers for the first time.

What Is the Gospel?

The New Testament is very clear on the details of the gospel message. In the following text, the Apostle Paul clearly lays out what the gospel entails as he reminds the Christians at Corinth what he had previously preached to them.

Christ for Post-Christians

> 1 Corinthians 15:1-8
>
> Now, brothers, I want to remind you of the gospel I preached to you, which you received and on which you have taken your stand. By this gospel you are saved, if you hold firmly to the word I preached to you. Otherwise, you have believed in vain. For what I received I passed on to you as of first importance: that Christ died for our sins according to the Scriptures, that he was buried, that he was raised on the third day according to the Scriptures, and that he appeared to Peter, and then to the Twelve. After that, he appeared to more than five hundred of the brothers at the same time, most of whom are still living, though some have fallen asleep. Then he appeared to James, then to all the apostles, and last of all he appeared to me also, as to one abnormally born.

The gospel is not complicated. It is something that can be easily communicated and understood by anyone:

1. Christ died for our sins. He bore the punishment for our sins.
2. He rose from the dead, signifying God's satisfaction with his sacrifice. That is the gospel, but it is not evangelism. Telling someone these facts is immensely important, but knowledge of the gospel requires a decision regarding these facts. That is evangelism.

Definitions of Evangelism

Christians see evangelism in differing ways and this leads to confusion as to its exact nature. There are several definitions of evangelism today:

1. Presence Evangelism: Presence evangelism is concerned with living the Christian life so that it will cause others to have an interest in the Christian faith. This form of evangelism puts emphasis on serving those without Christ. This takes the form of feeding the hungry, caring for the sick, and

helping the marginalized in society. Presence evangelism waits for the right opportunity to share the gospel with others. But this is incomplete evangelism.

2. Proclamation Evangelism: This type of evangelism believes good deeds are not enough; people must hear and understand the gospel. Proclamation means you tell people the gospel in such a way that they understand it. But this type of evangelism is not sufficient.

3. Persuasion Evangelism: This style of evangelism encourages the person to make a decision for Christ. A person not only must hear and understand the gospel; they also must be given the opportunity to make a decision to either accept or reject it. They must understand that a decision to accept the truth of the gospel is necessary for salvation. The third definition of evangelism is the task of the post-Christian Bible discussion group. Since Christ is presented as a living Savior, guests should be urged to make a decision. This is true evangelism. People need more than simply head knowledge of the gospel message; they need encouragement to make a decision for Christ. Evangelism is not just feeding the hungry or loving the marginalized in our society. These actions may be necessary to earn the right to share the gospel, but they alone are not sufficient for true evangelism.

Romans 10:5–13

Moses describes in this way the righteousness that is by the law: "The man who does these things will live by them." But the righteousness that is by faith says: "Do not say in your heart, 'Who will ascend into heaven?' " (that is, to bring Christ down) "or 'Who will descend into the deep?' " (that is, to bring Christ up from the dead). But what does it say? "The word is near you; it is in your mouth and in your heart," that is, the word of faith we are proclaiming: That if you confess with your mouth, "Jesus is Lord," and believe in your heart that God raised him from the dead, you will be saved. For it is with your heart that you believe and are justified, and it is with your mouth that you confess and are saved. As the Scripture says, "Anyone who trusts in him will never be put to shame." For there is no difference between Jew and Gentile—the same Lord is Lord of all and richly blesses all who call on him, for, "Everyone who calls on the name of the Lord will be saved."

When a person is confronted with the need to believe, the Bible says they must believe the gospel. The gospel *requires* a cognitive action—a response. This is the goal and reason for the Bible discussion group. At some point, guests not only must know the gospel, they must respond to it. Some Christians are confused about this. They think that as long as a person hears the gospel that is evangelism. However, the person of Christ always evokes a response, a decision. After learning about him, who he is, and what he says about himself, a decision is required (John 10:1–21; Acts 2:36–40). There may be apprehension and fear of rejection on the part of the leader. In response to fearful Christians Jesus says, "I am with you always" (Matthew 28:20). Be brave and confident; Jesus is with you. Do not be afraid of asking for a response. This is what Jesus has called you to do. When is the task of evangelism finished? The task is accomplished when, having understood that Jesus died for their sins, people choose to accept or reject Christ as Savior.

Evangelistic Planning

The Bible discussion group meetings require prayer and planning. The goal is to find passages and develop questions that eventually lead to a decision. This does not mean that everything will go as planned. There may be some hiccups along the way, such as when I was asked about the serpent lifted up in the wilderness. However, if the passage plan is laid out from beginning to end, along with appropriate questions, it will be easier to get back on track.

Imagine you are meeting for five sessions concluding with a follow-up activity:

- First Meeting - Introduction
- Second Meeting
- Third Meeting
- Fourth Meeting
- Fifth Meeting - Decision
- Outside Activity

How do you get from the "Introduction" at the first meeting to the "Decision" at the fifth meeting? The following is a sample of how you can set up your passage plan to lead to a decision point:

1. First Meeting: John 3:16. This verse has already been discussed. It introduces both Christ and the gospel at the outset and brings up the concept of belief. As previously stated, it is likely that some, if not all, of the three always-asked questions will come up.

2. Second Meeting: Romans 3:23-24. This passage is important because it introduces the universality of sinfulness. From the Bible's point of view, everyone is a sinner and needs salvation. The leader should be prepared with other passages that speak to what sin is. What is so significant about this verse is that it juxtaposes sinful man with the requirements of the glory of God.

3. Third Meeting: Romans 6:23. This passage introduces the penalty of sin. It is important because post-Christians do not believe they are sinners and do not understand the eternal consequences of sin. This verse also echoes back to John 3:16 and the concept of eternal life.

4. Fourth Meeting: Romans 5:8. This verse helps clear up what it means that Christ died for us. Remember, post-Christians

will not understand what the expression "Christ died for us" means. Guests must understand that Christ died in our place. He took the punishment that we deserved upon himself. I have heard many responses to the question, "What does it mean that Christ died for us?" The majority of responses were that he died as an example of how to love people. This response falls far short of a correct understanding of why Christ died for sinners. Leaders should not be discouraged if guests do not completely understand the meaning of the Lord's sacrifice. It may take time for the Holy Spirit to communicate exactly what it means. In one discussion group I led, eleven people responded that they thought Jesus died as an example of love. One woman, however, responded that she thought it meant more than that. She later became a Christian.

5. Fifth Meeting: Romans 10:9–11. This passage explains what faith is and defines evangelism. In order to be saved, guests must believe that Jesus died for their sins and simply say, "Yes, I believe that Jesus died for me." The leader must not be fearful of asking if they wish to believe now. Simply ask the whole group if they are now ready to believe that Jesus died for their sins. Do not be surprised if no one wants to voice his or her belief at that point. Remember, they have heard the gospel for the first time and they may want to think about it. On the other hand, some might respond. As previously stated, post-Christians must hear the gospel several times from different sources before they make a decision. This takes time. After the leader has asked the group to respond, he or she should give a short summary or overview of the passages that were discussed and thank everyone for participating. At the end, invite everyone to the chosen follow-up activity and then find out if anyone would like to continue getting together. If they are interested, then set up a time to discuss which topics interest them and decide on a time and place. Leaders use the same format as before:

discover what questions the guests may have and find where the Bible answers these questions.

Keep in contact with those in the group, even if they choose not to continue. Invite them to a "church retreat without church" where they can have more exposure to Christians. Chapter 8 explains how your church can become involved in providing opportunities for post-Christians to become involved with the Christian community.

7

Launching a Discussion Group —an Action Plan

Now that you are familiar with the material, it is time to make a decision regarding founding and leading a Bible discussion group for post-Christians. The first step is determining whether God is calling you to do this. If you felt excited about the principles set forth in this book, and thought, "I want to do this. I can do this!," this may indicate that God is calling you to start a group. God has already commanded you to "go and make disciples," so there is no need to ask if God wants you to witness for Jesus. The only question is whether God is calling you to witness for him in the particular format of a discussion group.

If you felt encouraged by what you read in this book, the next step is to meet with your pastor or ministry staff and your discipleship group to explain to them that you feel like God wants you to do this type of ministry. Ask for their thoughts and ask if they feel you are qualified. If they feel you need some work, then set up a spiritual growth plan to help you grow where needed. If they encourage you to start a discussion group that is a good sign that God wants you to get involved. These people know your strengths

Launching a Discussion Group—an Action Plan

and weaknesses and are your best source for determining if you are qualified to begin this work. If you are married, then the support of your spouse is necessary. If all these things come together, rest assured that God wants you to get started. Remember, you do not have to be a theologian or biblical scholar to lead a discussion group.

The next step is to find someone to work with you. Ask someone in your discipleship group and/or your spouse if they want to help. Be sure to share the material is this book with them. Take as much time as you need to make sure your coworker(s) understand the unique characteristics of such a discussion group. After this, you are ready to begin inviting people to come to the first meeting. If you do not know any post-Christians well enough to invite, then take the steps outlined in chapter 3.

Finally, a crucial step is to get right with God by confessing any sin in your life and ask the Holy Spirit to guide you. Pray for God's leading, care, and protection in all aspects of preparation. Ask God to use his Word to speak to the hearts of the people you invite. You will be amazed at how the Holy Spirit works through the Bible.

Here is a prayer you might want to pray:

> Thank you God that you have chosen me to reach those who do not know you. Please forgive me of my sin and fill me with your Holy Spirit. I want to be controlled by the Holy Spirit and lead a life pleasing to you. Help me to always confess my sins and renew my commitment to you. Help me to be aware of persons you bring across my path and give me wisdom to know how to relate to each one. May the Holy Spirit have total freedom to work in my heart and in the hearts of each guest at the discussion group meeting. Even if no one immediately accepts Christ, I will praise you for using me to share the gospel with these people for the first time. Please continue to work in each person's life. In Jesus name I pray, amen.

Post-Christian Bible discussion groups are not something you do just once. They should be an ongoing part of your life and ministry. Please plan time to do at least one discussion group each year. The number of times you host a group depends on the extent to which you or your friends come into contact with post-Christians and subsequently build relationships. Developing relationships takes time, of course. However, if you plan well in advance and put a discussion group on your calendar, you will remain sensitive to people with whom you come into contact, realizing that God is at work in the life of each person. Remember, God desires each person to come to faith.

> 2 Peter 3:9
>
> The Lord is not slow in keeping his promise, as some understand slowness. He is patient with you, not wanting anyone to perish, but everyone to come to repentance.

8

The Church and Post-Christians

Does the American church need to change in its response to the post-Christian culture? If so, what needs to change, and how? We must provide opportunities for incorporating non-Christians into the life of the community of believers. This is something I learned while ministering with German evangelical churches. These churches recognize and allow avenues where people—even not-yet-Christians—can become involved with the church. This does not mean they have leadership or decision-making roles, but rather they can take part in the group life of the church. Likewise, the American church can also discover ways to reach post-Christians. The changes I am suggesting may be difficult and greeted with skepticism, but are necessary if the church is to be viable in this post-Christian atmosphere. They will work in tandem with the Bible discussion groups and with the "church retreat without church."

If it takes several years for a post-Christian to come to faith, then there need to be ways that post-Christians can and will maintain contact with the church community. There must be a way to introduce them to Christianity without having to invite them to an "evangelistic event." Non-Christians need to be shown, not just told. Post-Christians want community. They want to belong to something and often want to serve those in need. This is where the church can involve those without Christ so they can see how Christians respond. This is where the church—without discounting Christian principles—can open up avenues for post-Christians to be introduced to the community of the faithful. Many churches have a variety of methods that use the talents and gifts of post-Christians in helping to fulfill needs of the local community. There are many things in which post-Christians can be involved:

1. Repairing cars of unwed mothers.
2. Serving food for the homeless.
3. Using their skills to repair church facilities.
4. Playing in the church band.
5. Teaching English to immigrants.
6. Helping plan church activities.

These are only suggestions. The point is to keep the long process of evangelism in view. Post-Christians must see how the church functions, which takes time and ingenuity on the part of the church. In all the examples I have seen, there has never been a case when a non-Christian wanted to be involved in church leadership or wanted to teach a Sunday school class. They only wanted to help with those things where their particular talents were appreciated. This might seem strange at first, but the church never hesitates to call a plumber to fix the plumbing. The question usually is not, "Is the plumber a Christian?" The main question is, "Can he fix the toilet?"

The missiologist Paul G. Hiebert describes two types of churches represented by the sketches below.[1]

---

1. Paul G. Hiebert, *Anthropological Reflections on Missiological Issues* (Grand Rapids: Baker, 1994), 116–17, 127–30.

The Church and Post-Christians

Figure 1

Figure 2

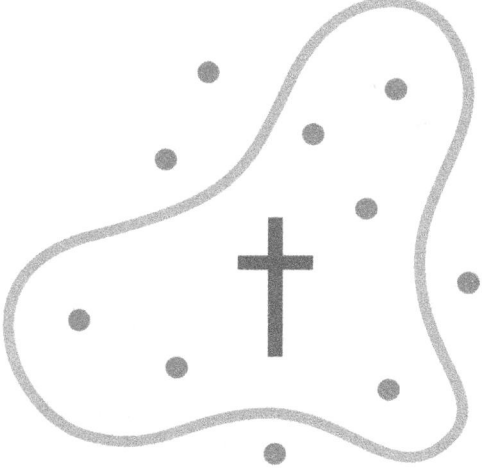

According to Hiebert, a clear boundary is important to both types of churches. However, they view non-Christians differently. The church in Figure 1 understands that those outside the circle need Christ. This church sees no distinction between people outside the circle and those inside. The attitude displayed is: trust Christ and become like us; you are either in or out. This church allows church participation only to those within the blue circle.

A clear boundary is also important to the church in Figure 2. However, this boundary is fluid, recognizing that there are fluctuations in a person's spiritual journey and where they are in relation to Christ. There is a clear line of who is and who is not a Christian, just as in the Figure 1. However, this church recognizes people are very different and some people are closer to receiving Christ than others. The church displayed in Figure 2 understands that there needs to be different approaches so that people will be drawn ever closer to trusting Christ. Although there is a clear line of demarcation, just as in the other church, they open up pathways where post-Christians can become involved in the community of Christians.

This may seem to be a radical approach, but post-Christian culture dictates that the gospel be contextualized in a way that it is understood. This means more than telling the gospel. It means opening up opportunities in the church community where post-Christians can be shown the gospel by observing the community of faith first-hand, as represented by the church in Figure 2. How this works in practice is as varied as the churches themselves. American churches should develop a plan that allows post-Christians to become involved with church activities without compromising the requirements of the church. As previously stated, this strategy should work together with Bible discussion groups. Those in the Bible discussion group need access to a church that includes more than simply the standard invitation to attend weekly services or an evangelistic outreach. They need to see first-hand how the church works. They need to be around Christians as much as possible. After hearing the gospel, it is necessary to provide specific openings where they can take part in activities exemplifying the normal

The Church and Post-Christians

lifestyle of those in the church. This provides them a chance to see how Jesus works through those he has called. They will see personally the challenges and joys of serving Christ by serving others. This may take a long time, but is the reality of the post-Christian culture confronting the American church. Are you and your church ready and willing to accept this challenge?

Please contact me for additional help or if you have any questions concerning the material presented. I would be happy to come share this material with your church or groups. You can contact me at christ4postchristians@gmail.com. Talk with your pastor about the evangelistic possibilities for post-Christians and how your church could engage in making post-Christian Bible discussion groups a part of its plan to fulfill the Great Commission.

www.ingramcontent.com/pod-product-compliance
Lightning Source LLC
Chambersburg PA
CBHW051707090426
42736CB00013B/2589